Robert Rose's
Favorite
COOKING FOR
KIDS

Robert
ROSE

ROBERT ROSE'S FAVORITE COOKING FOR KIDS

Canadian Cataloguing in Publication Data

Main entry under title:

Robert Rose's favorite cooking for kids

Includes index.

ISBN 0-7788-0015-6

1. Cookery.   I. Title: Cooking for kids.

TX652.R623 1999   641.5'622   C99-931248-0

DESIGN, EDITORIAL & PRODUCTION: MATTHEWS COMMUNICATIONS DESIGN INC.
PHOTOGRAPHY: MARK T. SHAPIRO

Cover photo: CHICKEN CHILI MACARONI (PAGE 26)

We acknowledge the financial support of the Government of Canada through the Book Publishing Industry Development Program (BPIDP) for our publishing activities.
Canadä

Published by: Robert Rose Inc. • 156 Duncan Mill Road, Suite 12
                  Toronto, Ontario, Canada   M3B 2N2   Tel: (416) 449-3535

Printed in Canada   1234567 BP 02 01 00 99

About this book

At Robert Rose, we're committed to finding imaginative and exciting ways to provide our readers with cookbooks that offer great recipes — and exceptional value. That's the thinking behind our "Robert Rose's Favorite" series.

Here we present over 50 favorite recipes just for kids — specially selected from a number of our bestselling full-sized cookbooks: Byron Ayanoglu's *New Vegetarian Gourmet*; Johanna Burkhard's *Comfort Food Cookbook* and *Fast & Easy Cooking*; Cinda Chavich's *Wild West Cookbook*; Rose Murray's *Quick Chicken*; Kathleen Sloan's *Global Grill*; and Rose Reisman's *Light Cooking, Light Pasta, Enlightened Home Cooking* and *Light Vegetarian Cooking*. We've also included recipes from our own *Robert Rose Book of Classic Pasta*.

We believe that it all adds up to great value for anyone who cooks for (or with!) kids.

For information about other books in our "Favorites" series, see page 96.

Contents

Snacks and Salads

Soups and Stews

Main Dishes

Cooking with Kids

Sweet Treats

Snacks and Salads

Serves 4

TIP

How to bake potatoes: Scrub baking potatoes (10 oz [300 g] each) well and pierce skins with a fork in several places to allow steam to escape.

To oven bake: Place in 400° F (200° C) oven for 1 hour or until potatoes give slightly when squeezed.

To microwave: Arrange potatoes in a circle, spacing 1 inch (2.5 cm) apart on roasting rack or on a paper towel in microwave oven. Microwave at High, turning over halfway through cooking time, until potatoes are just tender when pierced with a skewer. Microwave cooking times at High: 1 potato, 4 to 5 minutes; 2 potatoes, 6 to 8 minutes; 4 potatoes, 10 to 12 minutes. When potatoes are cooked, wrap individually in foil for moist potatoes or a towel for slightly dry. Let stand 5 minutes.

FROM
The Comfort Food Cookbook
by Johanna Burkhard

Beef-Stuffed Spuds

PREHEAT OVEN TO **400° F (200° C)**
SHALLOW BAKING DISH

4	large potatoes (about 10 oz [300 g] each)	4
8 oz	lean ground beef *or* ground veal	250 g
1/3 cup	finely chopped onions	75 mL
1	clove garlic, minced	1
1 tsp	Worcestershire sauce	5 mL
	Salt and pepper	
1/2 cup	sour cream *or* plain yogurt *or* buttermilk (approximate)	125 mL
2 tbsp	chopped parsley	25 mL
1 cup	shredded Cheddar cheese	250 mL

1. Bake or microwave potatoes as directed (see Tip, at left).

2. In a large nonstick skillet over medium–high heat, cook beef, breaking up with back of spoon, for 4 minutes or until no longer pink.

3. Reduce heat to medium. Add onions, garlic and Worcestershire sauce; season with salt and pepper. Cook, stirring often, for 4 minutes or until onions are softened.

4. Cut warm potatoes into half lengthwise. Carefully scoop out each potato, leaving a 1/4-inch (5 mm) shell; set aside.

5. In a bowl mash potatoes with a potato masher or fork; beat in enough sour cream to make smooth. Stir in beef mixture, parsley and half the cheese; season to taste with salt and pepper. Spoon into potato shells; top with remaining cheese.

6. Arrange in baking dish; bake in preheated oven for 15 minutes or until cheese is melted. Alternatively, place on microwave-safe rack or large serving plate; microwave at Medium-High for 5 to 7 minutes or until heated through and cheese melts.

Italian Pizza Egg Rolls

Makes 9

TIP

Children devour these tasty egg rolls. Double the recipe if necessary.

Ground chicken or veal can replace beef.

Cheddar cheese can replace mozzarella for a more intense flavor.

Roll the wrappers any way that's easy. Wetting the edges of the wrappers with water may help secure roll.

MAKE AHEAD

Prepare these up to 1 day ahead and keep refrigerated; add 5 minutes to cooking time.

These can also be prepared and frozen for up to 1 month.

PREHEAT OVEN TO 425° F (220° C)
BAKING SHEET SPRAYED WITH VEGETABLE SPRAY

1 tsp	vegetable oil	5 mL
1 tsp	minced garlic	5 mL
1/4 cup	finely chopped carrots	50 mL
1/4 cup	finely chopped onions	50 mL
1/4 cup	finely chopped green peppers	50 mL
3 oz	lean ground beef	75 g
1/2 cup	tomato pasta sauce	125 mL
1/2 cup	grated mozzarella cheese	125 mL
1 tbsp	grated Parmesan cheese	15 mL
9	egg roll wrappers (5 1/2 inches [13 cm] square)	9

1. In a nonstick skillet sprayed with vegetable spray, heat oil over medium heat. Add garlic, carrots and onions; cook for 8 minutes or until softened and browned. Add peppers; cook 2 minutes longer. Add beef; cook, stirring to break up, for 2 minutes or until no longer pink. Remove from heat; stir in tomato sauce, mozzarella and Parmesan cheeses.

2. Keeping rest of wrappers covered with a cloth to prevent drying out, place one on work surface with a corner pointing towards you. Place 2 tbsp (25 mL) filling in center. Fold lower corner up over filling, fold the 2 side corners in over filling and roll bundle away from you. Place on prepared pan; repeat until all wrappers are filled. Bake for 14 minutes or until browned, turning pizza rolls halfway through cooking time.

FROM
Rose Reisman's
Enlightened Home Cooking

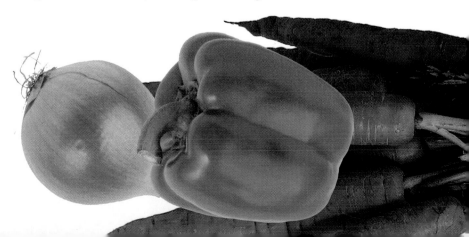

Caesar Tortilla Pizzas

Serves 4

I tried this pizza at the Planet Hollywood restaurant in Manhattan; this low-fat version is, I think, even more delicious than the original.

TIP

Try using pita bread instead of tortillas.

MAKE AHEAD

Prepare pizzas early in day and bake just before serving.

PREHEAT OVEN TO 400° F (200° C)
BAKING SHEET

Sauce

1	egg yolk	1
2 tbsp	grated Parmesan cheese	25 mL
2 tsp	freshly squeezed lemon juice	10 mL
1 tsp	minced garlic	5 mL
1/2 tsp	Dijon mustard	2 mL
2 tbsp	olive oil	25 mL
4	small flour tortillas (6-inch [15 cm]) *or* 2 large (10-inch [25 cm])	4

Toppings

1 cup	diced seeded plum tomatoes	250 mL
3/4 cup	shredded part-skim mozzarella cheese (about 3 oz [75 g])	175 mL
2 tbsp	grated Parmesan cheese	25 mL
1/2 cup	chopped romaine lettuce	125 mL

1. In a bowl whisk together egg yolk, 2 tbsp (25 mL) Parmesan cheese, lemon juice, garlic and mustard. Gradually add olive oil, whisking constantly. Place tortillas on baking sheet; divide sauce among tortillas, spreading to the edges.

2. Divide tomatoes, mozzarella and remaining Parmesan among tortillas.

3. Bake in preheated oven for 12 to 14 minutes or until cheese melts and tortillas start to brown. Top with lettuce; slice into triangles. Serve immediately.

FROM
Rose Reisman's
Light Vegetarian Cooking

Serves about 2

I developed this crunchy wing recipe for children's lunch boxes in a Canadian Living article, but it's a good quick supper item. Feel free to double the recipe as you'll find adults love them too!

MAKE AHEAD
Wings can be coated, covered and refrigerated for up to 4 hours before baking. Bring to room temperature for 30 minutes before cooking.

SHOPPING TIP
To save time, look for separated wings in the supermarket.

If buttermilk is unavailable, combine 1/4 cup (50 mL) sweet milk with 1 tsp (5 mL) vinegar; let stand for 15 minutes.

Reserve wing tips for stock or soup.

FROM
Quick Chicken
by Rose Murray

Kids' Wings

PREHEAT OVEN TO 425° F (220° C)
FOIL-LINED BAKING SHEET, GREASED

1 lb	chicken wings, separated at joints, tips removed	500 g
1/2 cup	all-purpose flour	125 mL
1 tbsp	wheat germ	15 mL
1 1/2 tsp	paprika	7 mL
1/2 tsp	dried marjoram	2 mL
1/2 tsp	dry mustard	2 mL
1/2 tsp	salt	2 mL
1/4 tsp	pepper	1 mL
1/4 cup	buttermilk	50 mL

1. In a plastic bag, shake together flour, wheat germ, paprika, marjoram, mustard, salt and pepper. Pour buttermilk into a shallow dish.

2. In batches, shake wings in flour mixture, shaking off excess back into bag. Dip into buttermilk; shake again in flour mixture. Arrange on prepared baking sheet. Bake in preheated oven for 30 minutes or until golden brown and no longer pink inside.

a b c d e f g

Crunchy Garlic Wings

Serves 4

These crisp wings are delicious by themselves or accompanied by the quick and easy Honey-Mustard Dipping Sauce. This simple recipe is sure to become a family hit.

SHOPPING TIP
Buy wings already separated to save time.

PREHEAT OVEN TO 425° F (220° C)
FOIL-LINED BAKING SHEET, GREASED

1/2 cup	dry bread crumbs	125 mL
1/2 cup	freshly grated Parmesan cheese	125 mL
1/4 cup	chopped fresh parsley	50 mL
1/4 tsp	pepper	1 mL

Honey-Mustard Dipping Sauce

1/4 cup	liquid honey	50 mL
4 tsp	Dijon mustard	20 mL
1/4 cup	butter	50 mL
4	cloves garlic, minced	4
3 lbs	chicken wings, halved at joint, tips removed	1.5 kg

1. In a bowl, mix together bread crumbs, cheese, parsley and pepper. Set aside.

2. In a bowl stir together honey and mustard until smooth.

3. In a small saucepan over low heat, melt butter with garlic.

4. Dip wings into butter mixture, then in bread crumb mixture, coating well. Arrange meaty-side down in a single layer on prepared baking sheet. Bake in preheated oven, turning once, for 25 minutes or until chicken is no longer pink inside. Serve hot with dipping sauce on side.

FROM
Quick Chicken
by Rose Murray

Baked French Wedge Potatoes

Serves 6

These "french fries" beat those cooked in lots of oil. Children and adults can't stop eating them!

TIP

For variety, try using different spices.

Potatoes should be firm, heavy and smooth. Keep in a cool ventilated place for 2 to 3 weeks to keep dry.

PREHEAT OVEN TO 375° F (190° C)
BAKING SHEET SPRAYED WITH VEGETABLE SPRAY

4	medium potatoes, unpeeled and scrubbed	4
2 tbsp	margarine, melted	25 mL
1/2 tsp	chili powder	2 mL
1/2 tsp	dried basil	2 mL
1 tsp	crushed garlic	5 mL
1 1/2 tsp	chopped fresh parsley	7 mL
1 tbsp	grated Parmesan cheese	15 mL

1. Place potatoes on baking sheet.
2. In a bowl combine margarine, chili powder, basil, garlic and parsley; brush half mixture over potatoes. Sprinkle with half of Parmesan; bake for 30 minutes. Turn wedges over; brush with remaining mixture and sprinkle with remaining cheese. Bake for 30 minutes longer.

FROM
Rose Reisman Brings Home
Light Cooking

Serves 4

Kids will love eating these "fingers" with their fingers; so why not make a whole meal of finger food, using the dip for raw vegetables as well.

MAKE AHEAD
The chicken fingers and honey dip can be made up to 4 hours ahead, covered and refrigerated.

FROM
Quick Chicken
by Rose Murray

Sesame Chicken Fingers with Honey Dip

PREHEAT OVEN TO 400° F (200° C)
FOIL-LINED COOKIE SHEET, GREASED

Honey Dip

1/3 cup	light mayonnaise	75 mL
3 tbsp	liquid honey	45 mL
1 tbsp	fresh lemon juice	15 mL
1/4 cup	light mayonnaise	50 mL
2 tbsp	Dijon mustard	25 mL
2 tbsp	fresh lemon juice	25 mL
1/3 cup	dry bread crumbs	75 mL
3 tbsp	sesame seeds	45 mL
1 tsp	dried Italian herb seasoning	5 mL
1 lb	skinless boneless chicken breasts, cut into strips 2 inches (5 cm) long by 1/2 inch (1 cm) wide	500 g

1. In a bowl prepare the dip by stirring together mayonnaise, honey and lemon juice until well combined. Refrigerate if making ahead.

2. In a bowl combine mayonnaise, Dijon mustard and lemon juice.

3. On waxed paper or in a bowl, combine bread crumbs, sesame seeds and Italian seasoning.

4. Coat chicken with mayonnaise mixture, then with bread crumb mixture. Place on prepared cookie sheet. Bake in preheated oven, turning once, for 15 to 20 minutes or until golden brown and chicken is no longer pink inside. Serve hot with the honey dip.

Serves 6

If anything signals the arrival of summer days and backyard barbecues, it's a trusty potato salad. My version goes beyond tossing potatoes with mayonnaise. In this recipe, warm potatoes are steeped in a tasty marinade before mayonnaise is introduced. The result? A summertime family favorite.

TIP

You can add 3 chopped hard-cooked eggs and 3/4 cup (175 mL) frozen peas, rinsed under hot water and drained well.

To hard-cook eggs: Pierce the wide end of egg with a pin or egg piercer. Place in saucepan and cover with cold water. Bring to a full rapid boil over high heat; remove from heat, cover and let stand for 15 minutes. Drain and run under cold water; crack shells while eggs are still warm to peel easily.

FROM
The Comfort Food Cookbook
by Johanna Burkhard

Best-Ever Potato Salad

2 lbs	new potatoes	1 kg
2 tbsp	red wine vinegar	25 mL
1 tbsp	Dijon mustard	15 mL
1	clove garlic, minced	1
4	green onions, chopped	4
2	stalks celery, diced	2
1/4 cup	chopped fresh parsley or dill	50 mL
1/2 cup	light mayonnaise	125 mL
1/4 cup	light sour cream or plain yogurt	50 mL
1/2 tsp	salt	2 mL
	Pepper	

1. In a saucepan cook whole potatoes in boiling salted water until just tender; drain. When cool enough to handle, peel and cut into 1/2-inch (1 cm) cubes. Place in serving bowl.

2. In a bowl stir together vinegar, mustard and garlic. Pour over warm potatoes; toss gently. Let cool to room temperature. Stir in onions, celery and parsley.

3. In a bowl combine mayonnaise, sour cream, salt and pepper. Fold into potato mixture until evenly coated. Refrigerate until serving time.

Caesar Salad

The king of tossed salads was named after a Tijuana restaurateur by the name of Caesar Cardini. Here, mayonnaise gives this classic salad an even creamier texture than the original.

TIP

Raw or coddled eggs are considered taboo in salads because they may contain salmonella bacteria. Mayonnaise is used instead.

Make sure salad greens are washed and dried thoroughly, preferably in a salad spinner, for best results.

Anchovy fillets are best, but 1 tbsp (15 mL) anchovy paste can be used instead.

FROM
The Comfort Food Cookbook
by Johanna Burkhard

1/3 cup	olive oil	75 mL
2 tbsp	mayonnaise	25 mL
2 tbsp	fresh lemon juice	25 mL
2 tbsp	water	25 mL
1 tsp	Dijon mustard	5 mL
2	cloves garlic, finely chopped	2
3	anchovy fillets, chopped	3
1/4 tsp	pepper	1 mL
1	large head Romaine lettuce, torn into bite-sized pieces	1
	GARLIC CROUTONS (recipe, next page)	
6	slices crisp bacon, crumbled	6
1/3 cup	freshly grated Parmesan cheese	75 mL
	Salt	

1. In a food processor, combine oil, mayonnaise, lemon juice, water, mustard, garlic, anchovy fillets and pepper; process until smooth and creamy.

2. Arrange lettuce in salad bowl; pour dressing over and toss lightly. Add croutons (see recipe, next page); sprinkle with crumbled bacon and Parmesan cheese. Toss again. If desired, season to taste with salt and pepper. Serve immediately.

Garlic Croutons

Homemade croutons make a definite flavor difference but 3 cups (750 mL) store-bought croutons work in a pinch.

PREHEAT OVEN TO 375° F (190° C)

4 cups	cubed crusty bread, cut into 1/2-inch (1 cm) pieces	1 L
2 tbsp	olive oil	25 mL
1	clove garlic, minced	1
2 tbsp	freshly grated Parmesan cheese	25 mL

1. Place bread cubes into a bowl. Combine oil and garlic; drizzle over bread cubes; toss. Sprinkle with Parmesan cheese; toss again. Arrange on baking sheet in single layer. Toast in preheated oven, stirring once, for 10 minutes or until golden.

Soups and Stews

Serves 6

I always look forward to late summer — when baskets of lush ripe tomatoes are the showpiece in outdoor markets — so I can make this silky smooth soup. In winter, vine-ripened greenhouse tomatoes make a good stand-in, particularly if you use a little tomato paste for extra depth. Just add 1 to 2 tbsp (15 to 25 mL) when puréeing soup.

Tip

A sunny window sill may seem like the ideal place to ripen tomatoes, but hot blistering sun can end up baking them instead.

To ripen, place tomatoes in a paper bag and leave on the counter at room temperature. Never store tomatoes in the fridge, it numbs their delicate flavor.

FROM
The Comfort Food Cookbook
by Johanna Burkhard

Creamy Tomato Soup

PREHEAT OVEN TO 400° F (200° C)
LARGE SHALLOW ROASTING PAN

1 tbsp	olive oil	15 mL
6	ripe tomatoes (2 lbs [1 kg]), cored and quartered	6
1	medium leek, white and light green part only, chopped	1
1	small onion, coarsely chopped	1
2	medium carrots, peeled and coarsely chopped	2
1	stalk celery (including leaves), chopped	1
2	large cloves garlic, sliced	2
1/2 tsp	salt	2 mL
1/4 tsp	pepper	1 mL
Pinch	nutmeg	Pinch
3 cups	chicken stock *or* vegetable stock (approximate)	750 mL
1 cup	light (15%) cream	250 mL
2 tbsp	chopped fresh herbs such as parsley, basil or chives	25 mL

1. Drizzle oil in bottom of roasting pan. Add tomatoes, leek, onion, carrot, celery and garlic; season with salt, pepper and nutmeg.

2. Roast in preheated oven, uncovered and stirring often, for 1 1/4 hours or until vegetables are very tender but not brown.

3. Add 2 cups (500 mL) stock to pan; purée mixture in batches, preferably in a blender or a food processor, until very smooth. Strain soup through a sieve into a large saucepan.

4. Add cream and enough of remaining stock to attain desired consistency. Season to taste with salt and pepper. Heat until piping hot (do not boil or soup may curdle). Ladle into warm bowls; sprinkle with fresh herbs.

Serves 4

This soothing and satisfying soup is made in minutes with chicken left from Sunday's roast.

Quick Chicken Noodle Soup

2 tbsp	butter	25 mL
1 cup	diced carrots	250 mL
4	green onions, sliced	4
5 cups	chicken stock	1.25 L
1	bay leaf	1
	Salt and pepper	
4 oz	very thin egg noodles	125 g
1 cup	diced cooked chicken	250 mL
1/2 cup	frozen peas	125 mL

1. In a saucepan melt butter over medium heat. Add carrots; cook for 3 minutes. Stir in green onions. Gradually stir in stock. Add bay leaf and salt and pepper to taste. Bring to a boil; reduce heat, cover and simmer for 3 to 5 minutes or until carrots are almost tender.

2. Return soup to a boil. Add noodles, chicken and peas; simmer, uncovered, for 3 to 5 minutes or until chicken is heated through and noodles are tender. Remove bay leaf; season to taste.

FROM
Quick Chicken
by Rose Murray

Cheese-Smothered Onion Soup

Serves 6

A good melting cheese with a nice nutty flavor (such as Gruyère or Raclette) works very well in this savory soup.

The assertive flavor of onions mellows and sweetens when cooked until golden.

TIP

Buy French bread 3 to 4 inches (8 to 10 cm) in diameter. Or, if using a thin baguette, use 2 slices of bread in each bowl.

The onion soup base can be made ahead and refrigerated for up to 5 days or frozen for up to 3 months.

Hate shedding tears when chopping onions? To minimize the weeping problem, use a razor-sharp knife to prevent loss of juices and cover the cut onions with a paper towel as you chop them to prevent the vapors from rising to your eyes.

FROM
The Comfort Food Cookbook
by Johanna Burkhard

DEEP OVENPROOF SOUP BOWLS
LARGE SHALLOW BAKING PAN

3 tbsp	butter	45 mL
8 cups	thinly sliced Spanish onions	2 L
1/4 tsp	dried thyme	1 mL
1/4 tsp	pepper	1 mL
2 tbsp	all-purpose flour	25 mL
6 cups	beef stock	1.5 L
1 tbsp	olive oil	15 mL
1	large garlic clove, minced	1
6	slices French bread, about 3/4-inch (2 cm) thick	6
2 cups	shredded Gruyère cheese	500 mL

1. In a Dutch oven or large heavy saucepan, heat butter over medium heat. Add onions, thyme and pepper; cook, stirring often, for 15 minutes or until onions are tender and a rich golden color. Blend in flour; stir in stock. Bring to a boil; stir until thickened. Reduce heat to medium-low; simmer, covered, for 15 minutes.

2. Meanwhile, position oven rack 6 inches (15 cm) from broiler; preheat broiler.

3. In a bowl combine olive oil and garlic; lightly brush over both sides of bread. Arrange on baking sheet; toast on both sides under broiler.

4. Place toasts in soup bowls; sprinkle with half the cheese. Arrange bowls in baking pan. Ladle hot soup into bowls; sprinkle with remaining cheese. Place under broiler for 3 minutes or until cheese melts and is lightly browned. Serve immediately.

abc defg

Serves 4

This quick pasta dish, cooked all in one pan, will be a real family pleaser.

VARIATION

For an Italian version, use Italian-style stewed tomatoes and substitute 1 tsp (5 mL) Italian herb seasoning for the chili powder as well as 1/2 cup (125 mL) Parmesan cheese for the Monterey Jack cheese. Serve with crusty rolls.

FROM
Quick Chicken
by Rose Murray

Chicken Chili Macaroni

1 lb	lean ground chicken	500 g
1	clove garlic, minced	1
1	can (14 oz [398 mL]) stewed tomatoes, preferably Mexican-style	1
1	can (14 oz [398 mL]) tomato sauce	1
1 tbsp	chili powder	15 mL
1/2 tsp	dried oregano	2 mL
1/2 tsp	ground cumin	2 mL
1 cup	elbow or wagon wheel macaroni	250 mL
1 cup	fresh or frozen cut green beans	250 mL
	Salt and pepper	
1 cup	shredded Monterey Jack or Cheddar cheese	250 mL

1. In a large skillet over medium-high heat, cook chicken and garlic, breaking it up with a wooden spoon, for 5 minutes or until chicken is no longer pink.

2. Stir in tomatoes, tomato sauce, chili powder, oregano and cumin. Bring to a boil. Stir in macaroni and green beans; bring back to a boil. Reduce heat to medium-low; cook, covered and stirring occasionally, for 15 minutes or until pasta and beans are tender. Season to taste with salt and pepper. Sprinkle with cheese.

Serves 4 to 6

Old-Fashioned Beef Stew

What's more comforting than a satisfying stew? You start feeling good the minute you set this one-pot dish to simmer on the stovetop. As the herb-infused aroma wafts through your kitchen the good feeling grows. The first forkful confirms that this stew is comfort food at its best. What's more, it can comfort you all over again the next day with easy-to-reheat leftovers. Delicious served with crusty bread to mop up the flavorful sauce.

TIP

To give your stew a rich, dark color, leave meat out of the refrigerator for 20 minutes; blot with paper towels before browning.

continues page 30...

FROM
The Comfort Food Cookbook
by Johanna Burkhard

1/4 cup	all-purpose flour	50 mL
1 tsp	salt	5 mL
1/2 tsp	pepper	2 mL
2 tbsp	vegetable oil (approximate)	25 mL
1 1/2 lbs	stewing beef, cut into 1 1/2-inch (4 cm) cubes	750 g
2	medium onions, chopped	2
3	cloves garlic, finely chopped	3
1 tsp	dried thyme	5 mL
1 tsp	dried marjoram	5 mL
1	bay leaf	1
1 cup	red wine *or* additional beef stock	250 mL
3 tbsp	tomato paste	45 mL
3 cups	beef stock (approximate)	750 mL
5	carrots, peeled and cut into 1 1/2-inch (4 cm) chunks	5
2	stalks celery, cut into 1 1/2-inch (4 cm) chunks	2
1 1/2 lbs	potatoes, peeled and quartered	750 g
12 oz	green beans, trimmed and cut into 1 1/2-inch (4 cm) chunks	375 g
1/4 cup	chopped fresh parsley	50 mL

1. Combine flour, salt and pepper in a heavy plastic bag. In batches, add beef to flour mixture; toss to coat well. Transfer beef to a plate; reserve remaining flour mixture.

2. In a Dutch oven, heat half the oil over medium-high heat; cook beef in batches, adding more oil as needed, until browned all over. Transfer to a plate.

3. Reduce heat to medium-low. Add onions, garlic, thyme, marjoram, bay leaf and remaining flour; cook, stirring, for 4 minutes or until softened. Add wine and tomato paste; cook, stirring to scrape up brown bits. Return beef and any accumulated juices to pan; pour in stock.

Recipe continues...

Cook beef in small batches for best browning and reheat pan before adding each new batch of meat. I find fresh meat browns better than frozen meat that has been defrosted.

4. Bring to a boil, stirring, until slightly thickened. Reduce heat to medium-low; simmer, covered, for 1 hour, stirring occasionally.

5. Add carrots, celery and potatoes to pan. Cover; simmer for 30 minutes.

6. Add green beans to stew; adding more stock to cover vegetables. Cover; simmer for 30 minutes or until vegetables are tender. Remove bay leaf; stir in parsley. Season to taste with salt and pepper.

Creamy Baked Beefaroni

PREHEAT OVEN TO 450° F (230° C)
9- BY 13-INCH (3 L) BAKING DISH SPRAYED WITH VEGETABLE SPRAY

Meat Sauce

1 tsp	vegetable oil	5 mL
2 tsp	minced garlic	10 mL
1 cup	chopped onions	250 mL
12 oz	lean ground beef	375 g
1 3/4 cups	tomato pasta sauce	425 mL
1/2 cup	beef or chicken stock	125 mL

Cheese Sauce

1 1/2 tbsp	margarine *or* butter	20 mL
1/4 cup	all-purpose flour	50 mL
2 cups	2% milk	500 mL
1 3/4 cups	beef or chicken stock	425 mL
1 cup	grated Cheddar cheese	250 mL
1 lb	penne	500 g
1/2 cup	grated mozzarella cheese	125 mL
2 tbsp	grated Parmesan cheese	25 mL

1. In a nonstick saucepan, heat oil over medium heat. Cook garlic and onions for 4 minutes or until softened. Add beef; cook, stirring to break up, for 4 minutes or until no longer pink. Add tomato sauce and stock; simmer, covered, for 10 minutes or until thickened. Set aside.

2. In saucepan, melt margarine over medium-low heat. Add flour; cook, stirring, for 1 minute. Gradually add milk and stock. Cook, stirring constantly, until sauce begins to boil. Reduce heat to low; cook for 5 minutes, stirring occasionally, until slightly thickened. Stir in Cheddar cheese; remove from heat. Combine cheese sauce with meat sauce; set aside.

3. In a large pot of boiling water, cook pasta according to package directions or until tender but firm; drain. Toss pasta with sauce; pour into prepared dish. Sprinkle with mozzarella and Parmesan cheeses; bake for 10 minutes or until bubbly on top.

Serves 6 to 8

Every cook has a special version of chili. Here's mine — it's meaty and nicely spiced with just the right amount of beans. Not everyone agrees that beans belong in a chili — witness the Texas version dubbed "bowl of red" — but I love the way the beans absorb the spices and rich tomato flavor.

TIP

The flavor of the chili hinges on the quality of chili powder used. Most powders are a blend of dried and ground mild chilies, as well as cumin, oregano, garlic and salt. Read the list of ingredients to be sure you're not buying one with starch and sugar fillers. Chili powder should not be confused with powdered or ground chilies of the cayenne pepper variety.

FROM
The Comfort Food Cookbook
by Johanna Burkhard

Amazing Chili

1 1/2 lbs	lean ground beef	750 g
2	medium onions, chopped	2
3	cloves garlic, finely chopped	3
2	stalks celery, chopped	2
1	large green bell pepper, chopped	1
2 tbsp	chili powder	25 mL
1 1/2 tsp	dried oregano	7 mL
1 1/2 tsp	ground cumin	7 mL
1 tsp	salt	5 mL
1/2 tsp	red pepper flakes, or to taste	2 mL
1	can (28 oz [796 mL]) tomatoes, chopped, juice reserved	1
1 cup	beef stock	250 mL
1	can (19 oz [540 mL]) pinto or red kidney beans, rinsed and drained	1
1/4 cup	chopped fresh parsley or coriander	50 mL

1. In a Dutch oven over medium-high heat, brown beef, breaking up with back of a spoon, for 7 minutes or until no longer pink.

2. Reduce heat to medium. Add onions, garlic, celery, green pepper, chili powder, oregano, cumin, salt and red pepper flakes; cook, stirring often, for 5 minutes or until vegetables are softened.

3. Stir in tomatoes with juice and stock. Bring to a boil; reduce heat. Simmer, covered and stirring occasionally, for 1 hour.

4. Add beans and parsley; simmer, covered, for 10 minutes.

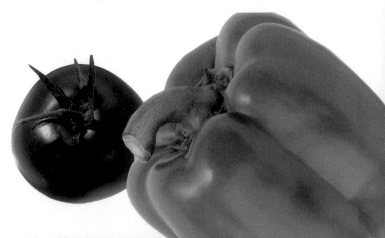

Spicy Meatball and Pasta Stew

Meatballs

8 oz	lean ground beef	250 g
1	egg	1
2 tbsp	ketchup or chili sauce	25 mL
2 tbsp	seasoned bread crumbs	25 mL
1 tsp	minced garlic	5 mL
1/2 tsp	chili powder	2 mL

Stew

2 tsp	vegetable oil	10 mL
1 tsp	minced garlic	5 mL
1 1/4 cups	chopped onions	300 mL
3/4 cup	chopped carrots	175 mL
3 1/2 cups	beef stock	875 mL
1	can (19 oz [540 mL]) tomatoes, crushed	1
3/4 cup	canned chickpeas, drained	175 mL
1 tbsp	tomato paste	15 mL
2 tsp	granulated sugar	10 mL
2 tsp	chili powder	10 mL
1 tsp	dried oregano	5 mL
1 1/4 tsp	dried basil	6 mL
2/3 cup	small shell pasta	150 mL

1. In a large bowl, combine ground beef, egg, ketchup, bread crumbs, garlic and chili powder; mix well. Form 1/2 tbsp (7 mL) mixture at a time into meatballs; place on baking sheet. Cover; set aside.

2. In a large nonstick saucepan, heat oil over medium heat. Add garlic, onions and carrots; cook for 5 minutes or until onions are softened. Stir in stock, tomatoes, chickpeas, tomato paste, sugar, chili powder, oregano and basil; bring to a boil. Reduce heat to medium-low; cook, covered, for 20 minutes. Bring to a boil; stir in pasta and meatballs. Simmer for 10 minutes or until pasta is tender but firm and meatballs are cooked through.

Main Dishes

Bet you didn't know that the banquet burger began life in Toronto, Canada! Invented by restaurant owner Francis Deck and originally dubbed the Forest Hill burger (after an upscale area of Toronto), it was created to boost flagging sales back in the 1940s. If you want to make this a truly Canadian burger, use back bacon in place of regular bacon.

Use a cheese grater to grate the peeled onion directly over the bowl.

The Great Canadian Banquet Burger

PREHEAT LIGHTLY GREASED GRILL TO HIGH

2 lbs	medium ground beef	1 kg
1 ½ tsp	salt	7 mL
1 tsp	freshly ground black pepper	5 mL
2 tbsp	Worcestershire sauce	25 mL
1	medium onion, grated	1
6	thin slices Cheddar cheese	6
12	slices cooked bacon	12
6	hamburger buns *or* kaiser rolls	6
6	lettuce leaves	6
6	thick slices tomato	6
	Onion, ketchup, mustard, mayonnaise and dill pickles	

1. In a bowl combine beef, salt, pepper, Worcestershire sauce and onion. Mix together until well blended. Shape into 6 equal-sized patties, about 1 inch (2.5 cm) thick.

2. Place patties on grill. Cook, turning once, 5 minutes per side for medium or until exterior of burger is nicely browned. Add cheese during last minute of cooking time.

3. Split buns; toast on grill. Assemble burgers by placing 1 patty on bottom of bun followed by 2 strips of bacon (or 1 piece cooked Canadian back bacon). Place a lettuce leaf and tomato slice on other side of bun. Serve with garnish at table.

FROM
The Global Grill
by Kathleen Sloan

Serves 6

Cowboy Steak

3 lbs	round steak, 3/4 inch (2 cm) thick, cut into 6 pieces	1.5 kg
2 cups	all-purpose flour	500 mL
1 tsp	salt	5 mL
1 tsp	freshly ground black pepper	5 mL
1	egg	1
1/4 cup	milk *or* 10% cream	50 mL
	Canola oil for frying	
2 tbsp	all-purpose flour	25 mL
2 cups	milk *or* 10% cream	500 mL
	Salt and pepper to taste	

1. In a shallow dish, combine 2 cups (500 mL) flour, salt and pepper; dip meat into flour mixture, coating well. Pound steak with a meat mallet to about 1/4- to 1/2-inch (5 mm to 1 cm) thickness; set aside. In a bowl whisk together egg and 1/4 cup (50 mL) milk.

2. Fill a large cast-iron frying pan 1/4 inch (5 mm) high with canola oil; heat over medium-high heat until sizzling. Dip meat into egg mixture, then into spiced flour, coating well. Cook steak, in two batches, for 1 to 2 minutes or until browned on one side. Turn meat carefully; brown other side. Reduce heat to medium; return all steak to pan. Add 3 tbsp (45 mL) water; cook, covered, for 8 minutes or until cooked through. Remove steak from pan; keep warm.

3. Add 2 tbsp (25 mL) flour to browned bits in pan; cook, stirring, for 1 minute. Gradually add 2 cups (500 mL) milk or cream; cook, stirring, until cream gravy is thick and smooth. Season to taste with salt and pepper; pour over steaks.

This dish is known as "chicken fried steak" in Texas, where they stir cream into the pan drippings to make a rich gravy. Texans, one Texas foodie remarked, need to have their chicken fried steak at least once a week and "only a rank degenerate would drive clear across Texas without stopping for a chicken fried steak." Likely left over from the days of long cattle drives, when steers killed on the trail were sinewy and tough, the steak benefits from being tenderized or pounded with flour and flavorings before cooking. Not a low-cal dish, but a traditional one on the prairies from Elko to Estevan.

FROM
The Wild West Cookbook
by Cinda Chavich

Kids' Favorite Spaghetti Pie

Leftover pasta in the fridge is perfect for this pizza-like supper dish that's especially appealing to the younger set.

TIP

It's easy to turn this recipe into a vegetarian dish — just omit the meat. Broccoli can be replaced by zucchini, bell peppers or whatever vegetables you have on hand.

PREHEAT OVEN TO 350° F (180° C)
9- OR 10-INCH (23 OR 25 CM) GLASS PIE PLATE, OILED

8 oz	mild or hot Italian sausages, casings removed *or* lean ground beef	250 g
2 cups	sliced mushrooms	500 mL
1	small onion, chopped	1
1	large clove garlic, finely chopped	1
1 1/2 tsp	dried oregano	7 mL
2 cups	tomato pasta sauce	500 mL
2 cups	small broccoli florets, rinsed	500 mL
3 cups	cooked spaghetti or any string pasta (6 oz [175 g] uncooked)	750 mL
1 1/2 cups	shredded part-skim mozzarella cheese	375 mL

1. In a saucepan over medium–high heat, cook sausage meat, breaking up with a wooden spoon, for 4 minutes or until no longer pink. Drain in sieve to remove any fat; return to saucepan. Add mushrooms, onion, garlic, and oregano; cook, stirring, for 3 minutes or until vegetables are softened. Add tomato pasta sauce; simmer, covered, for 10 minutes.

2. Place broccoli in a covered casserole dish. Microwave at High for 2 to 2 1/2 minutes or until bright green and almost tender. Rinse under cold water to chill; drain.

3. Arrange spaghetti in pie plate. Spread with meat sauce; top with broccoli and sprinkle with cheese. Bake for 25 to 30 minutes or until cheese is melted. Cut into wedges and serve.

FROM
Fast & Easy Cooking
by Johanna Burkhard

Zesty Barbecued Spareribs

Serves 4

"You've got to put your rib recipe in your cookbook," advised my son, whose favorite dinner request is a plate of these succulent ribs. So here it is. And since the only way to eat ribs is with your fingers, be sure to have plenty of napkins handy.

TIP

Ribs are great on the barbecue, too. Partially cook ribs in oven for 45 minutes as directed in recipe. Complete cooking on grill over medium-low flame, basting often with the sauce.

Tabasco is the most familiar brand of hot sauce, so we've used it here. However, supermarket shelves now boast a large assortment of hot sauces — so experiment with various sauces available and add according to taste.

FROM
The Comfort Food Cookbook
by Johanna Burkhard

PREHEAT OVEN TO 375° F (190° C)
SHALLOW ROASTING PAN OR BROILER PAN, WITH RACK

3 to 4 lbs	pork spareribs	1.5 to 2 kg
	Salt and pepper	
1 cup	prepared chili sauce *or* ketchup	250 mL
1/2 cup	honey	125 mL
1	small onion, finely chopped	1
2	cloves garlic, minced	2
2 tbsp	Worcestershire sauce	25 mL
2 tbsp	lemon juice	25 mL
1 tbsp	Dijon mustard	15 mL
1 tsp	Tabasco or other hot pepper sauce (or to taste)	5 mL
1	lemon, cut into wedges	1

1. Place ribs on rack in roasting pan; season with salt and pepper. Cover with foil. Roast in preheated oven for 45 minutes.

2. In a small saucepan, combine chili sauce, honey, onion, garlic, Worcestershire sauce, lemon juice, mustard and Tabasco sauce; bring to a boil. Reduce heat; simmer, stirring occasionally, for 10 to 15 minutes or until slightly thickened.

3. Remove foil; brush ribs generously on both sides with sauce. Roast, uncovered, for 45 minutes, brushing generously every 15 minutes with sauce, or until spareribs are nicely glazed and tender.

4. Cut into serving-size portions; serve with any remaining sauce and lemon wedges.

Serves 4

This dish sounds grown up — but kids love the apples and sweet sauce!

TIP
Apple cider gives the sauce a more intense flavor than apple juice does.

MAKE AHEAD
Assemble and refrigerate chicken rolls early in day. Brown and bake just before serving. Prepare and refrigerate sauce, adding more stock if too thick when reheating.

FROM
Rose Reisman Brings Home
Light Cooking

Chicken Breasts Stuffed with Apple and Almonds

PREHEAT OVEN TO 400° F (200° C)
BAKING DISH SPRAYED WITH NONSTICK VEGETABLE SPRAY

1 1/2 tsp	margarine	7 mL
1/2 cup	chopped peeled apple	125 mL
1 tbsp	almond slices	15 mL
1/4 tsp	cinnamon	1 mL
4	boneless skinless chicken breasts	4
1	egg white	1
1/2 cup	dry bread crumbs	125 mL
1 1/2 tsp	vegetable oil	7 mL

Sauce

1 tbsp	margarine	15 mL
1 tbsp	all-purpose flour	15 mL
3/4 cup	apple juice or cider	175 mL
1/4 cup	chicken stock	50 mL
1/4 tsp	cinnamon	1 mL
1 1/2 tsp	brown sugar	7 mL

1. In a nonstick skillet, heat margarine over medium heat. Add apple, almonds and cinnamon; cook for 5 minutes or until apple is tender.

2. Place chicken between 2 sheets of waxed paper; pound until flattened. Top evenly with apple mixture; carefully roll up, securing with toothpicks. Dip into egg white, then into bread crumbs.

3. In a large nonstick skillet, heat oil over medium–high heat. Add chicken; cook just until browned on all sides. Place in baking dish.

4. Sauce: In a small saucepan, heat margarine over medium heat. Add flour; cook, stirring, for 1 minute. Add apple juice, stock, cinnamon and sugar; cook, stirring, for 3 minutes or until thickened. Pour sauce over chicken; bake, covered, for 10 to 15 minutes or until chicken is no longer pink inside.

Serves 4 to 6

Best-Ever Macaroni and Cheese

TIP

The most common error in cooking pasta is not using enough water to boil the pasta — with the result that it cooks unevenly and sticks together.

How to cook 1 lb (500 g) of pasta: Using a large pot, bring 16 cups (4 L) water to a full rolling boil. Add 1 tbsp (15 mL) salt (this is important for flavor) and all the pasta at once. Do not add oil. Start stirring immediately to prevent pasta from sticking.

Cover with a lid to return water quickly to a full boil, then uncover and stir occasionally. Taste to see if pasta is *al dente*. Drain immediately. Never rinse pasta — this chills it and removes the coating of starch that helps sauce cling to pasta. Return to pot or place in a large warmed serving bowl; add the sauce and toss until well-coated. Serve immediately

FROM
The Comfort Food Cookbook
by Johanna Burkhard

PREHEAT OVEN TO 375° F (190° C)
8-CUP (2 L) DEEP CASSEROLE DISH, BUTTERED

3 tbsp	butter	45 mL
1/4 cup	all-purpose flour	50 mL
1	bay leaf	1
3 cups	milk	750 mL
1 tbsp	Dijon mustard	15 mL
	Salt and cayenne pepper	
2 cups	shredded Cheddar cheese, preferably aged	500 mL
2 cups	elbow macaroni	500 mL
1 tbsp	butter	15 mL
1 cup	soft bread crumbs	250 mL

1. In a large saucepan, heat butter over medium heat. Add flour and bay leaf; cook, stirring, for 30 seconds. Pour in 1 cup (250 mL) milk, whisking constantly until mixture comes to a boil and thickens. Pour in rest of milk in a slow stream, whisking constantly, until sauce comes to a full boil and is smooth. Whisk in mustard.

2. Reduce heat to low; stir in cheese until melted. Remove bay leaf; season to taste with salt and a dash of cayenne pepper. Remove from heat.

3. Meanwhile, in a large pot of boiling salted water, cook macaroni for 8 minutes or until just tender. (Do not overcook; pasta continues to cook in sauce.) Drain well. Add to cheese sauce; stir to coat well. Spoon into prepared casserole dish.

4. In a bowl, microwave remaining 1 tbsp (15 mL) butter on High for 20 seconds or until melted. Toss with bread crumbs; sprinkle over pasta. Bake in preheated oven for 25 minutes or until bubbly and lightly browned.

Serves 4

Chicken Tortillas

TIP

Boneless turkey breast, pork or veal scallopini can replace chicken.

The cheese adds a creamy texture to the tortillas. Mozzarella cheese can also be used.

MAKE AHEAD

Prepare filling early in the day; gently reheat before stuffing tortillas. Add extra stock if the sauce is too thick.

PREHEAT OVEN TO 375° F (190° C)
BAKING SHEET SPRAYED WITH VEGETABLE SPRAY

6 oz	skinless, boneless chicken breast, diced	150 g
1 tsp	vegetable oil	5 mL
1 tsp	crushed garlic	5 mL
1 cup	chopped onions	250 mL
1/2 cup	finely chopped carrots	125 mL
1 cup	tomato pasta sauce	250 mL
1 cup	canned red kidney beans, drained	250 mL
1/2 cup	chicken stock	125 mL
1 tsp	chili powder	5 mL
8	6-inch (15 cm) flour tortillas	8
1/2 cup	shredded Cheddar cheese (optional)	125 mL

1. In a nonstick skillet sprayed with vegetable spray, cook chicken over high heat for 2 minutes or until no longer pink inside. Remove from skillet; set aside.

2. Reduce heat to medium; add oil to pan. Cook garlic, onions and carrots, stirring often, for 10 minutes or until browned and softened. Add water if vegetables start to burn. Add tomato sauce, beans, stock and chili powder; cook for 10 to 12 minutes or until carrots are tender and mixture has thickened. Stir in chicken; remove from heat.

3. Scoop 1/3 cup (75 mL) mixture onto each tortilla. Sprinkle with cheese (if using) and roll up. Place on prepared baking sheet; bake for 10 minutes or until heated through.

FROM
Rose Reisman's
Enlightened Home Cooking

Amazing Turkey Enchiladas

Serves 6

Instead of turning turkey leftovers into a week's worth of cold sandwiches, whip up this fast-fix dinner with loads of family appeal.

TIP

You can assemble this dish 1 day ahead of baking; just top with salsa and cheese prior to popping in the oven.

Cooked chicken or 1 1/2 cups (375 mL) small cooked shrimp can be used instead of turkey.

PREHEAT OVEN TO 350° F (180° C)
13- BY 9-INCH (3 L) BAKING DISH, OILED

1/2 cup	light cream cheese	125 mL
1/2 cup	plain low-fat yogurt *or* light sour cream	125 mL
2 cups	cooked turkey, cut into strips	500 mL
3	green onions, finely chopped	3
2	tomatoes, seeded and diced	2
1/4 cup	chopped fresh coriander or parsley	50 mL
6	8-inch (20 cm) flour tortillas	6
1 1/2 cups	mild or medium salsa	375 mL
1 cup	shredded Cheddar cheese or Monterey Jack cheese	250 mL

1. Place cream cheese in a large bowl; microwave at Medium for 1 minute to soften. Stir well. Add yogurt, turkey, green onions, tomatoes and coriander.

2. Spread about 1/2 cup (125 mL) turkey mixture down center of each tortilla; roll up. Arrange tortillas in a single layer, seam-side down, in baking dish. Spread with salsa; sprinkle with cheese. Bake for 30 to 35 minutes or until heated through. Sprinkle with extra chopped coriander, if desired.

To Microwave
Do not sprinkle with cheese. Cover dish with waxed paper; microwave at Medium-High for 7 to 9 minutes or until heated through. Sprinkle with cheese; microwave at High for 1 minute or until cheese melts.

FROM
Fast & Easy Cooking
by Johanna Burkhard

Roasted Chicken Fajitas

Serves 4

Roasting the chicken strips and vegetables in the oven not only adds flavor to the fajitas, but is a fast and easy way of making them.

VARIATION
Sautéed Chicken Fajitas
Instead of roasting the chicken and vegetables, sauté the chicken strips in half the oil over medium-high heat for 3 to 5 minutes or until browned. Remove from the pan; add remaining oil and vegetables. Cook for 5 minutes, stirring often.

SHOPPING TIP
Buy chicken strips that are already cut and packaged for stir-fries.

FROM
Quick Chicken
by Rose Murray

PREHEAT OVEN TO 400° F (200° C)
LARGE SHALLOW ROASTING PAN, GREASED

1 lb	skinless boneless chicken breasts, cut crosswise into 5 or 6 strips	500 g
2 tbsp	vegetable oil	25 mL
1 tbsp	fresh lime juice	15 mL
1 tsp	chili powder	5 mL
1/2 tsp	ground cumin	2 mL
2	large onions, cut into wedges	2
2	large red bell peppers, cut into wide strips	2
	Salt and pepper	
8	large flour tortillas	8
1 cup	shredded lettuce (optional)	250 mL
2	avocados, peeled and sliced	2
	Tomato salsa	
	Sour cream	

1. In a bowl combine chicken, half the oil, lime juice, chili powder and cumin; set aside.

2. In prepared roasting pan, combine onions and peppers. Drizzle with remaining oil; sprinkle with salt and pepper. Add chicken mixture, stirring to combine well; spread out in pan. Roast in preheated oven, stirring once or twice, for 20 to 25 minutes or until chicken is no longer pink inside and vegetables are tender.

3. Meanwhile, wrap tortillas tightly in foil. Place in preheated oven for 10 minutes to heat.

4. Transfer chicken and vegetables to a warm platter; serve with tortillas, lettuce, avocados, salsa and sour cream. Have each diner spoon chicken mixture into a tortilla; top with accompaniments and roll up to eat.

Crunchy Cheese and Herb Drumsticks

Serves 4

TIP
Use bran flakes instead of natural bran; it has a sweetness that children love.

MAKE AHEAD
Coat the drumsticks up to 1 day ahead. They can be baked a few hours in advance and then gently reheated. Great for leftovers.

PREHEAT OVEN TO 400° F (200° C)
BAKING SHEET SPRAYED WITH VEGETABLE SPRAY

1 1/2 cups	bran or corn flakes cereal	375 mL
1 1/2 tbsp	fresh chopped parsley	20 mL
2 1/2 tbsp	grated Parmesan cheese	35 mL
1 tsp	minced garlic	5 mL
3/4 tsp	dried basil (or 1/2 tsp [2 mL] dried)	4 mL
1/2 tsp	chili powder	2 mL
1/8 tsp	ground black pepper	0.5 mL
1	egg	1
2 tbsp	milk or water	25 mL
8	skinless chicken drumsticks	8

1. In a food processor combine bran flakes, parsley, Parmesan, garlic, basil, chili powder and pepper; process into fine crumbs. Set aside.

2. In a bowl whisk together egg and milk. Dip each drumstick into egg wash, then roll in crumbs; place on prepared baking sheet. Bake, turning halfway, for 35 minutes or until browned and chicken is cooked through.

FROM
Rose Reisman's
Enlightened Home Cooking

Chicken and Bean Burritos

Serves 4

A fun supper for kids, these burritos are quick and easy to make with inexpensive ground chicken.

MAKE AHEAD
Chicken and bean filling can be made up to 1 day ahead, covered and refrigerated. Reheat in a skillet over low heat.

The mixture can also be frozen for up to 2 months. Thaw in the refrigerator and reheat.

1 tbsp	vegetable oil	15 mL
1 lb	ground chicken	500 g
1	small red bell pepper, chopped	1
2	green onions, sliced	2
2 tsp	ground cumin	10 mL
1/2 tsp	dried oregano	2 mL
1/4 tsp	hot pepper flakes (or to taste)	1 mL
1	can (19 oz [540 mL]) black beans or kidney beans, rinsed and drained	1
1 cup	bottled salsa	250 mL
2 tbsp	chopped fresh coriander	25 mL
	Salt	
6	10-inch (25 cm) flour tortillas	6
	Additional salsa, sour cream and sliced green onions	

1. In a large heavy skillet, heat oil over medium-high heat. Add chicken, pepper and onions; cook, stirring often, for 7 minutes, breaking up chicken with spoon.

2. Stir in cumin, oregano and hot pepper flakes. Add beans, salsa and coriander; simmer until most liquid is evaporated, mashing beans against side of skillet. If desired, season to taste with salt and hot pepper flakes.

3. Meanwhile, in a covered skillet over medium-high heat, set tortillas on a rack over 1/2 inch (1 cm) water; simmer for 30 seconds.

4. Place 1 tortilla on work surface; mound one-sixth chicken mixture on lower half, leaving a 1/2-inch (1 cm) border along edges. Roll up tightly, folding in sides to enclose filling. Repeat with remaining tortillas. Spoon additional salsa, sour cream and green onions on top.

FROM
Quick Chicken
by Rose Murray

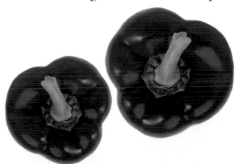

Ground Chicken Pizza

Serves 3 or 4

This easy pizza has lots of kid appeal. For pineapple aficionados, top the chicken with pineapple tidbits before sprinkling the last of the cheese.

SHOPPING TIP

Pizza dough is often available in the freezer section of supermarkets. Pre-made uncooked crusts can be found in the cooler section where there are store-made pizzas. You can also stop by your local pizzeria and buy 1 lb (500 g) dough.

FROM
Quick Chicken
by Rose Murray

PREHEAT OVEN TO 500° F (260° C)

2 tbsp	olive oil	25 mL
12 oz	lean ground chicken	375 g
8 oz	mushrooms, sliced	250 g
Half	green bell pepper, cut into chunks	Half
1	12-inch (30 cm) uncooked pizza crust *or* 1 lb (500 g) pizza dough	1
8 oz	mozzarella or provolone cheese, shredded	250 g
1 tsp	dried Italian herb seasoning	5 mL
1	can (7 1/2 oz [213 mL]) pizza sauce	1

1. In a large skillet heat half the oil over medium-high heat. Add chicken; cook for 5 minutes, breaking up with a spoon. Add mushrooms; cook for 5 minutes. Add green pepper; cook for 1 minute.

2. Brush pizza crust with some of the remaining oil; sprinkle with half the cheese. In a bowl, combine herb seasoning with sauce; spread over pizza. Arrange chicken mixture on top; sprinkle with remaining cheese. Drizzle with remaining oil. Bake in preheated oven for 12 to 15 minutes or until crust is golden brown.

Pasta Shells Stuffed with Cheese in a Creamy Tomato Sauce

Serves 4 or 5

TIP

Ricotta cheese is available in 5% and 10% fat — to reduce fat use the 5%

Always cook an additional pasta shell or two; it will give you a sample to taste for doneness, and you will have extra if any tear.

PREHEAT OVEN TO 375° F (190° C)
13- BY 9-INCH (3 L) BAKING DISH, GREASED

1/4 cup	whipping (35%) cream	50 mL
8 oz	jumbo pasta shells *or* 12 manicotti shells	250 g
1 cup	ricotta cheese	250 mL
1/2 cup	grated Parmesan cheese	125 mL
1/4 cup	finely chopped chives or green onions	50 mL
1/4 cup	shredded Havarti, brick or fontina cheese	50 mL
2	egg yolks	2
2 cups	prepared tomato sauce	500 mL
1/3 cup	grated Parmesan cheese Chopped chives	75 mL

1. Pour cream into prepared baking dish.

2. In a large pot of boiling salted water, cook pasta shells for 8 to 10 minutes or until tender; drain. Rinse under cold water; drain. Set aside.

3. In a bowl combine ricotta cheese, Parmesan cheese, chives, Havarti cheese and egg yolks. Stuff pasta shells with mixture; place in baking dish. Pour tomato sauce over shells; sprinkle with Parmesan. Cover dish tightly with aluminum foil.

4. Bake in preheated oven for 20 minutes or until heated through. Serve sprinkled with chopped chives.

FROM
The Robert Rose Book of
Classic Pasta

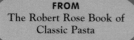

Serves 8

Sweet and Sour Chicken Meatballs over Rice

TIP

If your kids don't like rice, serve this dish over 1 lb (500 g) spaghetti. Also, feel free to omit the onions. If children like pineapple, add 1 cup (250 mL) pineapple cubes (canned or fresh) at the end of the cooking time.

MAKE AHEAD

Make up to 2 days ahead; reheat before serving. Can be frozen for up to 6 weeks. Great for leftovers.

12 oz	ground chicken	375 g
1/4 cup	finely chopped onions	50 mL
2 tbsp	ketchup	25 mL
2 tbsp	bread crumbs	25 mL
1	egg	1
2 tsp	olive oil	10 mL
2 tsp	minced garlic	10 mL
1/3 cup	chopped onions	75 mL
2 cups	tomato juice	500 mL
2 cups	pineapple juice	500 mL
1/2 cup	chili sauce	125 mL
2 cups	white rice	500 mL

1. In a bowl combine chicken, onions, ketchup, bread crumbs and egg; mix well. Form each 1 tbsp (15 mL) mixture into a meatball; set aside.

2. In a large saucepan, heat oil over medium heat. Add garlic and onions; cook for 3 minutes or until softened. Add tomato juice, pineapple juice, chili sauce and meatballs. Simmer, covered, for 30 to 40 minutes or until meatballs are tender.

3. Meanwhile, bring 4 cups (1 L) water to boil; add rice. Reduce heat; simmer, covered, for 20 minutes or until liquid is absorbed. Remove from heat; let stand for 5 minutes, covered. Serve meatballs and sauce over rice.

FROM
Rose Reisman's
Enlightened Home Cooking

Cooking with Kids

Greek Chicken Pita Sandwiches

Serves 4

When I'm in the mood for an easy dinner, this is what I make. These sandwiches beat fast food hands down.

TIP

A combination of lemon juice, garlic and oregano is the classic marinade for souvlaki. I also use it as a quick marinade combined with 1 tbsp (15 mL) olive oil to brush-over chicken breasts and pork loin chops on the barbecue.

1 lb	skinless boneless chicken breasts, cut into very thin strips	500 g
1 tbsp	freshly squeezed lemon juice	15 mL
1	large clove garlic, minced	1
3/4 tsp	dried oregano	4 mL
1/4 tsp	salt	1 mL
1/4 tsp	pepper	1 mL
2 tsp	olive oil	10 mL
1	small red onion, halved lengthwise and thinly sliced	1
1	red or green bell pepper, cut into 2-inch (5 cm) strips	1
4	pitas (7-inch [18 cm]), halved to make pockets	4
3/4 cup	tzatziki sauce	175 mL
4 cups	shredded romaine lettuce	1 L
2	tomatoes, cut into wedges	2

1. In a bowl combine chicken, lemon juice, garlic, oregano, salt and pepper; marinate at room temperature for 10 minutes.

2. In a large nonstick skillet, heat oil over high heat. Cook chicken, stirring, for 2 to 3 minutes or until no longer pink. Add onion and bell pepper; cook, stirring, for 2 minutes or until vegetables are softened.

3. Wrap pitas in paper towels; microwave at Medium for 1 1/2 minutes or until warm. Spoon chicken mixture into pita halves; top with tzatziki sauce, shredded lettuce and tomato wedges.

FROM
Fast & Easy Cooking
by Johanna Burkhard

Serves 6

Chicken-Chutney Kabobs

A spicy yogurt coating renders the chicken moist and delicious in this interesting dinner-on-a-stick. It's great for the family — but could certainly be company fare.

MAKE AHEAD

The chicken can be marinated up to 8 hours ahead in the refrigerator. Bring to room temperature for 30 minutes before cooking.

GREASE GRILL AND PREHEAT TO MEDIUM-HIGH

1 cup	mango chutney, large bits chopped	250 mL
1/2 cup	plain yogurt	125 mL
1 tsp	ground cumin	5 mL
1/2 tsp	turmeric *or* curry powder	2 mL
1 tbsp	olive oil	15 mL
1 1/2 lbs	boneless chicken breasts or thighs, cut into 1 1/2–inch (4 cm) pieces	750 g
1	onion, cut into wedges	1
1	red bell pepper, cut into 1-inch (2.5 cm) squares	1
2	small zucchini, cut into 1-inch (2.5 cm) slices	2

1. In a bowl combine chutney, yogurt, cumin, turmeric and oil. Add chicken; marinate at room temperature for 30 minutes.

2. Reserving the marinade, thread chicken pieces alternately with onion, red pepper and zucchini onto 6 long skewers. Place on grill (or under the broiler); cook, turning often and brushing with marinade, for 15 minutes or until chicken is no longer pink inside.

FROM
Quick Chicken
by Rose Murray

Serves 4

Kids love simple dishes like this one, with its straightforward flavors — so simple that even young cooks can make it.

TIP

This recipe also works well with a whole cut-up chicken or bone-in chicken breasts. With its tang of lemon and sweetness of honey, this dish is sure to become a family favorite.

Just-For-Kids Honey Lemon Chicken

PREHEAT OVEN TO 350° F (180° C)
13- BY 9-INCH (3 L) BAKING DISH

4	chicken legs, skinned	4
2 tbsp	honey	25 mL
2 tsp	grated lemon zest	10 mL
1 tsp	freshly squeezed lemon juice	5 mL
1	large clove garlic, minced	1
1/4 tsp	salt	1 mL
1/4 tsp	pepper	1 mL

1. Arrange chicken in baking dish. In a bowl combine honey, lemon zest, lemon juice, garlic, salt and pepper; spoon over chicken.

2. Bake in oven, basting once, for 45 to 55 minutes or until juices run clear when chicken is pierced.

FROM
Fast & Easy Cooking
by Johanna Burkhard

Makes 4 burgers

If burgers are starting to become mundane, put some excitement in those patties. Instead of cheese on top of the burger, put shredded cheese right into the ground meat mixture for moist burgers with a twist. Mama would be pleased.

TIP

For an easy vegetable topping, cut green or red bell peppers and a large red onion into rounds. Brush lightly with olive oil and grill alongside burgers.

Mama's Italian Cheeseburgers

PREHEAT LIGHTLY GREASED GRILL TO MEDIUM-HIGH

1/4 cup	tomato pasta sauce	50 mL
1/4 cup	grated or minced onion	50 mL
1	clove garlic, minced	1
1/4 tsp	dried basil or oregano	1 mL
1/4 tsp	salt	1 mL
1/4 tsp	pepper	1 mL
3/4 cup	shredded part-skim mozzarella or Fontina cheese	175 mL
1/3 cup	dry seasoned bread crumbs	75 mL
1 lb	lean ground beef	500 g
4	hamburger buns, split and lightly toasted	4

1. In a bowl combine pasta sauce, onion, garlic, basil, salt and pepper. Stir in cheese and bread crumbs; mix in beef. Shape into four 3/4-inch (2 cm) thick patties.

2. Place patties on grill; cook, turning once, for 12 to 14 minutes or until meat is no longer pink. Serve in buns.

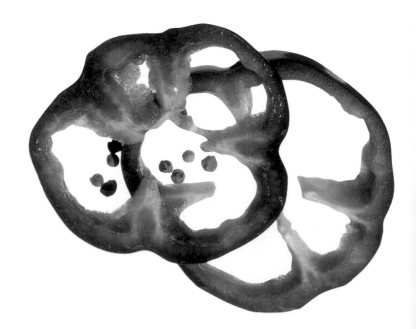

FROM
Fast & Easy Cooking
by Johanna Burkhard

Serves 4

Taco Pitas

Once the meat is browned, it takes no time to add the beans and seasonings to make the tasty filling. Aside from being lower in fat, I find pita breads make much better containers than taco shells, which tend to crumble when you bite into them and cause the filling to spill out.

Double the recipe and freeze extras for another meal.

The only major chore left to getting supper ready is shredding the cheese and preparing the vegetable garnishes — simple tasks that young cooks can handle.

TIP
To heat pitas, wrap in foil and place in a 350° F (180° C) oven for 15 to 20 minutes. Or wrap 4 at a time in paper towels and microwave at High for 1 to 1 1/2 minutes.

FROM
Fast & Easy Cooking
by Johanna Burkhard

8 oz	lean ground beef	250 g
1	small onion, finely chopped	1
1	large garlic clove, minced	1
2 tsp	chili powder	10 mL
2 tsp	all-purpose flour	10 mL
1/2 tsp	dried oregano	2 mL
1/2 tsp	ground cumin	2 mL
Pinch	cayenne pepper	Pinch
1/2 cup	beef stock	125 mL
1	can (19 oz [540 mL]) pinto, black or red kidney beans, rinsed and drained	1
6	pitas (7-inch [18 cm]), halved to form pockets and warmed	6
	Salsa, shredded lettuce, tomato wedges, bell pepper strips, shredded mozzarella or Cheddar cheese	

1. In a large nonstick skillet over medium-high heat, cook beef, breaking up with back of a spoon, for 4 minutes or until no longer pink.

2. Reduce heat to medium. Add onion, garlic, chili powder, flour, oregano, cumin and cayenne pepper. Cook, stirring often, for 5 minutes or until onions are softened.

3. Add stock; cook, stirring, until slightly thickened. Stir in beans; cook 2 minutes or until heated through.

4. Spoon 1/4 cup (50 mL) mixture into pita pockets; top with salsa, lettuce, tomato, pepper and cheese.

VARIATION

Sloppy Joe Pitas
Increase beef to 1 lb (500 g). Omit beans and add 1 can (7 1/2 oz [213 mL]) tomato sauce; cook 3 minutes longer or until sauce is slightly thickened.

Serves 4

I've taken the classic BLT and fashioned it into a wrap, adding fresh basil to the mayonnaise for a thoroughly modern twist.

TIP

If tomatoes aren't fully ripened, place in a paper bag to sit on your counter for a day a two. The ethylene gas given off by the tomatoes speeds up the ripening process.

Never store tomatoes in the fridge – the cold temperature numbs their sweet flavor.

A sunny windowsill may seem like a good place to ripen tomatoes, but the hot sun often bakes rather than ripens them.

FROM
Fast & Easy Cooking
by Johanna Burkhard

It's a BLT Wrap!

8	slices bacon, cut into quarters	8
1/3 cup	light mayonnaise	75 mL
2 tbsp	chopped fresh basil (or 1/2 tsp [2 mL] dried)	25 mL
4	flour tortillas (8-inch [20 cm])	4
2	large tomatoes, cut into half crosswise, seeds squeezed out and thinly sliced	2
4 cups	shredded romaine lettuce	1 L

1. Place bacon on a microwave-safe rack or on a large plate lined with paper towels; loosely cover with another layer of paper towels. Microwave at High for 5 minutes or until cooked and almost crisp; set aside to cool.

2. In a bowl combine mayonnaise and basil. Spread over tortillas leaving a 1-inch (2.5 cm) border around edge. Layer tortillas with tomato slices, lettuce and bacon. Fold 1-inch (2.5 cm) of right and left sides of tortilla over filling; starting from bottom, roll tortillas around filling. Serve immediately or wrap in plastic and store in the refrigerator for up to 1 day.

VARIATION

Club Wrap

Cut 2 grilled or cooked chicken breasts into thin strips. Spread tortillas with basil mayonnaise; layer with tomato, lettuce, chicken and bacon. Roll tortillas as directed.

*"Let's order pizza!"
The next time you
hear this request
from your kids,
assemble these
ingredients and
get them cooking.*

TIP

This recipe is the
perfect solution to
deal with the odd
bits of vegetables,
cheese and deli
left in the fridge by
week's end. Vary
the toppings
according to what
you have on hand
including sliced
pepperoni,
chopped ham or
broccoli.

Four 7-inch
(18 cm) pitas or
6 split English
muffins can also
be used. Reduce
the baking time to
10 minutes. If
necessary, arrange
on 2 baking
sheets; rotate
halfway during
baking so the
bread bakes
evenly.

FROM
The Comfort Food Cookbook
by Johanna Burkhard

Flatbread Pizzas

PREHEAT OVEN TO 400° F (200° C)
BAKING SHEET

1 tbsp	vegetable oil or olive oil	15 mL
1	small onion, thinly sliced	1
1	clove garlic, minced	1
1 cup	sliced mushrooms	250 mL
1	small green or red bell pepper, cut into thin strips	1
1/2 tsp	dried basil	2 mL
1/2 tsp	dried oregano	2 mL
1	12-inch (30 cm) prebaked pizza base *or* 9- by 12-inch (23 by 30 cm) focaccia	1
1/2 cup	pizza sauce (approximate)	125 mL
2 cups	shredded cheese, (mozzarella Fontina, provolone etc.)	500 mL

1. In a large nonstick skillet, heat oil over medium–high heat. Add onions, garlic, mushrooms, bell pepper, basil and oregano; cook, stirring, for 4 minutes or until softened.

2. Arrange pizza shell on baking sheet; spread with pizza sauce. Top with vegetables and shredded cheese.

3. Bake in preheated oven for 20 to 24 minutes or until cheese is melted.

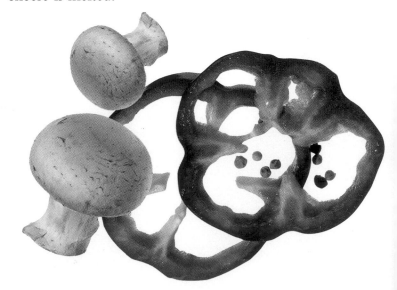

Beef and Sausage Sloppy Joes

Serves 6 to 8

TIP

Children often prefer a smoother sauce. If too chunky, run through the food processor.

If a livelier taste is desired, use spicy sausage.

This recipe can also be used as a pasta sauce.

MAKE AHEAD

Can be made up to 2 days ahead or frozen for up to 3 weeks. Great as leftovers.

2 tsp	vegetable oil	10 mL
1 cup	chopped onions	250 mL
2 tsp	minced garlic	10 mL
8 oz	lean ground beef	250 g
8 oz	mild Italian sausage, chopped and casings removed	250 g
4 cups	chopped fresh tomatoes *or* 1 can (28 oz [796 mL]) tomatoes drained and chopped	1 L
1 1/2 tsp	dried basil	7 mL
1 tsp	chili powder	5 mL
1/2 tsp	dried oregano	2 mL
2 tbsp	grated Parmesan cheese (optional)	25 mL

1. In a large nonstick skillet, heat oil over medium heat; add onions and garlic. Cook for 4 minutes or until softened. Add ground beef and sausage; cook for 5 minutes, breaking up meat with a spoon, or until no longer pink. Drain off excess fat.

2. Add tomatoes, basil, chili powder and oregano; bring to a boil. Reduce heat to low; simmer uncovered for 30 minutes, stirring occasionally. Serve over toasted hamburger buns. Sprinkle with Parmesan cheese if desired.

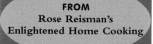

FROM
Rose Reisman's
Enlightened Home Cooking

Bagel Garlic Bread

**PREHEAT OVEN TO 350° F (180° C)
BAKING SHEET**

2	bagels	2
1 tbsp	margarine, melted	15 mL
1/2 tsp	crushed garlic	2 mL
1 1/2 tsp	grated Parmesan cheese	7 mL
1 tbsp	chopped fresh parsley	15 mL

1. Slice each bagel into 6 very thin rounds.

2. In a bowl combine margarine, garlic, cheese and parsley. Brush over bagel rounds.

3. Bake in preheated oven for 10 to 14 minutes or until crisp.

FROM
Rose Reisman Brings Home
Light Cooking

Makes 2 dozen cookies

These big cookies, chock-full of grains and seeds, make a filling breakfast on the run. The recipe comes from the Heartland Country Store in Calgary.

Nutricookies

PREHEAT OVEN TO 350° F (180° C)
BAKING SHEETS, GREASED

2 cups	butter, at room temperature	500 mL
2 cups	brown sugar	500 mL
4	eggs	4
1/4 cup	buttermilk	50 mL
2 cups	whole wheat flour	500 mL
2 cups	unbleached flour	500 mL
4 cups	rolled oats (large flake oats)	1 L
1/4 cup	bran	50 mL
2 tsp	baking soda	10 mL
1 tbsp	baking powder	15 mL
1 1/2 cups	chocolate chips	375 mL
1/2 cup	slivered almonds	125 mL
1/4 cup	raw sunflower seeds	50 mL

1. In a bowl cream together butter and sugar. Beat in eggs, one at a time; add buttermilk.

2. In another bowl combine whole wheat flour, unbleached flour, oats, bran, baking soda, baking powder, chocolate chips, almonds and sunflower seeds until well mixed. Add to creamed mixture; mix until well blended.

3. Scoop about 1/2 cup (125 mL) dough onto baking sheet; flattening into a cookie shape (these cookies don't spread much). Bake for 15 to 20 minutes or until golden brown.

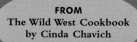

FROM
The Wild West Cookbook
by Cinda Chavich

Cream Cheese-Filled Brownies

PREHEAT OVEN TO 350° F (180° C)
8-INCH (2 L) SQUARE BAKING DISH, SPRAYED WITH VEGETABLE SPRAY

Filling

4 oz	light cream cheese, softened	125 g
2 tbsp	granulated sugar	25 mL
2 tbsp	2% milk	25 mL
1 tsp	vanilla extract	5 mL

Cake

1 cup	packed brown sugar	250 mL
1/3 cup	light sour cream	75 mL
1/4 cup	vegetable oil	50 mL
1	egg	1
1	egg white	1
3/4 cup	all-purpose flour	175 mL
1/2 cup	cocoa	125 mL
1 tsp	baking powder	5 mL

1. **Filling:** In a food processor or in a bowl with an electric mixer, beat together cream cheese, sugar, milk and vanilla until smooth. Set aside.

2. **Cake:** In a bowl whisk together brown sugar, sour cream, oil, whole egg and egg white. In another bowl stir together flour, cocoa and baking powder. Add liquid ingredients to dry, blending just until mixed.

3. Pour half cake batter into prepared pan. Spoon filling on top; spread with a wet knife. Pour remaining batter into pan. Bake 20 to 25 minutes or until just barely loose at center.

FROM
Rose Reisman's
Light Vegetarian Cooking

Makes 40 cookies

Peanut Butter Fudge Cookies

TIP
Chopped dates
can replace
raisins.

Use a natural
peanut butter,
smooth or chunky.

MAKE AHEAD
Cookies never last
long, but these
can be made up
to 1 day ahead,
kept tightly cov-
ered in a cookie
jar or tin.

Prepare cookie
dough and freeze
for up to 2 weeks.

PREHEAT OVEN TO 350° F (180° C)
BAKING SHEETS SPRAYED WITH VEGETABLE SPRAY

1/4 cup	softened margarine or butter	50 mL
1/3 cup	peanut butter	75 mL
3/4 cup	granulated sugar	175 mL
1/4 cup	brown sugar	50 mL
1	egg	1
1 tsp	vanilla	5 mL
1 cup	all-purpose flour	250 mL
1/4 cup	cocoa	50 mL
1 tsp	baking powder	5 mL
1/4 cup	2% yogurt	50 mL
3/4 cup	raisins	175 mL
3 tbsp	chocolate chips	45 mL

1. In a large bowl cream together margarine, peanut butter, sugar and brown sugar. Add egg and vanilla; beat well.

2. In another bowl combine flour, cocoa and baking powder; add to peanut butter mixture, stirring just until combined. Add yogurt, raisins and chocolate chips. Drop by heaping teaspoonful (15 mL) onto prepared sheets 2 inches (5 cm) apart; press down slightly with back of fork. Bake for 12 minutes or until firm to the touch and slightly browned.

a b c d e f g h

FROM
Rose Reisman's
Enlightened Home Cooking

Sweet Treats

Serves 6

Wild Berry Shortcake

Wild berries include wild strawberries and raspberries, low-bush and high-bush cranberries, chokecherries, Nanking cherries and wild currants, and have been used by natives and settlers for hundreds of years. Find your own favorite patch or look for these wild delicacies at summer farmer's markets.

PREHEAT OVEN TO 425° F (220° C)
BAKING SHEET

2 lbs	fresh mixed berries (blueberries, wild strawberries, saskatoons, raspberries, etc.)	1 kg
1/4 cup	apple juice	50 mL
1/4 cup	granulated sugar	50 mL

Biscuit

1/2 cup	all-purpose flour	125 mL
1/2 cup	whole wheat flour	125 mL
1/4 cup	ground pecans or walnuts	50 mL
1/2 cup	brown sugar	125 mL
1/2 tsp	salt	2 mL
2 tsp	baking powder	10 mL
1 tsp	baking soda	5 mL
1/4 cup	butter	50 mL
1/2 cup	yogurt	125 mL
1/2 tsp	vanilla	2 mL
1 cup	whipping (35%) cream, whipped with a little sugar *or* 1 cup [250 mL] low-fat vanilla yogurt	250 mL

1. In a bowl combine fruit with juice and sugar; set aside.

2. Meanwhile, in another bowl, stir together all-purpose flour, whole wheat flour, pecans, brown sugar, salt, baking powder and baking soda. Cut in butter with a pastry cutter, forming coarse crumbs. Add yogurt and vanilla; stir to combine.

3. Place biscuit dough on a slightly floured surface; pat to a 1-inch (2.5 cm) thickness. Cut into 2-inch (5 cm) circles with a biscuit cutter. Brush with some milk; sprinkle with granulated sugar. Bake in preheated oven for 10 to 15 minutes or until golden; cool slightly.

4. Cut biscuits in half horizontally; place bottom half on dessert plate. Top with half berry mixture and whipped cream. Repeat with remaining biscuits, berries and cream.

FROM
The Wild West Cookbook
by Cinda Chavich

Kids' Favorite Chocolate Pudding

1/3 cup	granulated sugar	75 mL
1/4 cup	cornstarch	50 mL
2 1/4 cups	milk	550 mL
1/3 cup	semi-sweet chocolate chips	75 mL
1 tsp	vanilla	5 mL

Why rely on expensive store-bought puddings when you can make nourishing home-made ones that take little time to make?

Milk puddings are also a great way to boost calcium intake.

1. In a medium-sized saucepan whisk together sugar and cornstarch; add milk, whisking until smooth. Place over medium heat; cook, stirring, for 5 minutes or until mixture comes to a full boil; cook for 15 seconds.

2. Remove from heat. Stir in chocolate chips and vanilla; blend until smooth. Pour pudding into individual serving dishes. Let cool slightly; cover surface with plastic wrap to prevent skins from forming on surface. Refrigerate.

TIP

Whole milk gives a creamier consistency than low-fat 1% or skim milk in this easy-to-make dessert.

If cooking pudding in the microwave, be sure to use a large bowl to prevent boil-overs.

Microwave method

In an 8-cup (2 L) glass bowl or casserole dish, whisk together sugar and cornstarch; add milk, whisking until smooth. Microwave at High for 3 minutes. Whisk well; microwave at High for 3 to 4 minutes, whisking every minute, or until pudding comes to a full boil and thickens. Stir in chocolate chips and vanilla.

VARIATION
Butterscotch Pudding
Cook pudding as directed. Substitute 1/2 cup (125 mL) butterscotch chips for the chocolate chips; reduce sugar to 1/4 cup (50 mL).

FROM
Fast & Easy Cooking
by Johanna Burkhard

Maple Custard with Fresh Fruit

Serves 4

Looking for an easy family-pleasing dessert? This one takes only a few minutes to prepare.

TIP

Any kind of fresh, frozen or drained canned fruit can be used. Maple syrup is preferred, but maple-flavored pancake syrup can be substituted.

1 1/4 cups	milk	300 mL
1/2 cup	maple syrup	125 mL
2	egg yolks	2
2 tbsp	cornstarch	25 mL
2	peaches, pears or bananas, peeled and sliced	2

1. In a saucepan add milk, maple syrup, egg yolks and cornstarch; whisk until smooth. Cook over medium-low heat, whisking constantly, for 2 to 4 minutes or until boiling and thickened.

2. Arrange fruit in 4 individual serving dishes; pour hot custard over. Refrigerate, covered, for 1 hour or until cool.

FROM
Fast & Easy Cooking
by Johanna Burkhard

Serves 16

TIP

Very ripe bananas can be kept frozen for up to 1 year.

Raisins can be replaced with chopped pitted dates, apricots or prunes.

A food processor can be used to mix the cake. Do not over-process.

MAKE AHEAD

Bake up to 2 days ahead. Freeze for up to 6 weeks.

FROM
Rose Reisman's
Enlightened Home Cooking

Carrot Cake with Cream Cheese Frosting

PREHEAT OVEN TO 350° F (180° C)
9-INCH (3 L) BUNDT PAN SPRAYED WITH VEGETABLE SPRAY

1/3 cup	margarine *or* butter	75 mL
1 cup	granulated sugar	250 mL
2	eggs	2
1 tsp	vanilla	5 mL
1	large ripe banana, mashed	1
2 cups	grated carrots	500 mL
2/3 cup	raisins	150 mL
1/2 cup	canned pineapple, drained and crushed	125 mL
1/2 cup	2% yogurt	125 mL
2 cups	all-purpose flour	500 mL
1 1/2 tsp	baking powder	7 mL
1 1/2 tsp	baking soda	7 mL
1 1/2 tsp	cinnamon	7 mL
1/4 tsp	nutmeg	1 mL

Icing

1/3 cup	light cream cheese, softened	75 mL
2/3 cup	icing sugar	150 mL
1 tbsp	2% milk	15 mL

1. In a bowl cream together margarine and sugar until smooth; add eggs and vanilla. Beat well (mixture may look curdled). Add banana, carrots, raisins, pineapple and yogurt; stir until well combined.

2. In a bowl stir together flour, baking powder, baking soda, cinnamon and nutmeg. Add to carrot mixture; stir just until combined. Pour into prepared pan; bake for 40 to 45 minutes or until cake tester inserted in center comes out clean. Let cool for 10 minutes; invert onto serving plate.

3. In a bowl with electric mixer or a food processor, beat together cream cheese, icing sugar and milk until smooth; drizzle over cake. If desired, decorate with grated carrots.

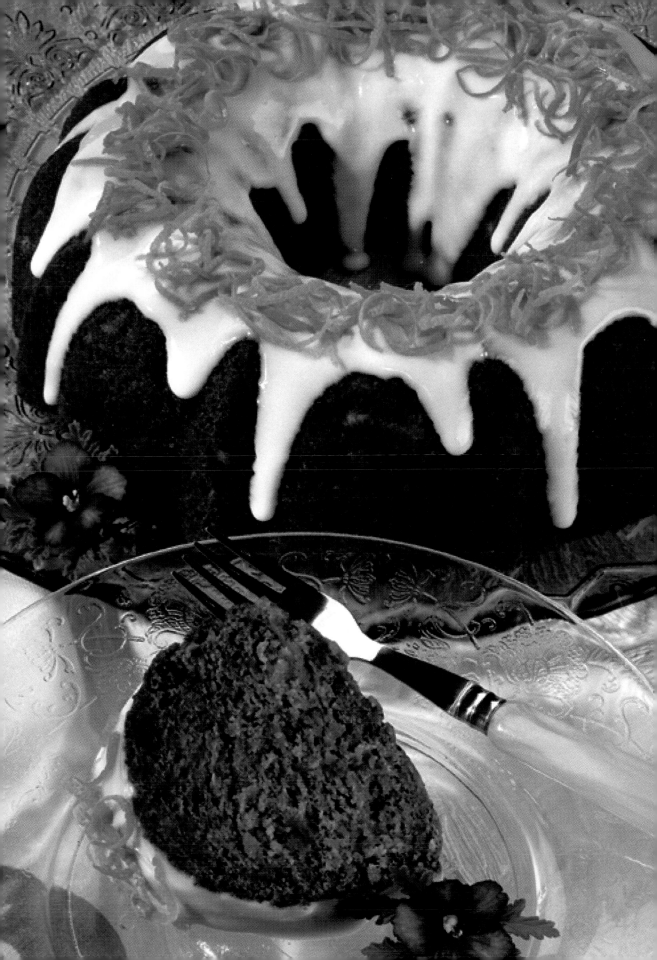

Farmhouse Apple Pie

Intimidated by the thought of making two-crust pies? Try this simple free-form pie – it only needs a single pie crust and looks like it came from a pastry shop.

TIP

Store-bought pastry for a single crust pie can be used instead of the suggested homemade pastry.

PREHEAT OVEN TO 375° F (190° C)
LARGE BAKING SHEET, LIGHTLY GREASED

Pastry

1 1/4 cups	all-purpose flour	300 mL
1 tbsp	granulated sugar	15 mL
Pinch	salt	Pinch
1/2 cup	butter, cut into pieces	125 mL
2 tbsp	cold water (approximate)	25 mL

Filling

4	apples (Golden Delicious, Spy Granny Smith etc.) peeled, cored and sliced	4
1/3 cup	granulated sugar	75 mL
1/4 cup	finely chopped pecans	50 mL
1/2 tsp	cinnamon	2 mL

1. Pastry: In a bowl combine flour, sugar and a generous pinch of salt. Cut in butter with pastry blender (or use fingertips) to make coarse crumbs. Sprinkle with enough water to hold dough together; gather into a ball. Flatten to a 5-inch (12 cm) circle; wrap in plastic wrap. Refrigerate for 30 minutes.

2. On a lightly floured board, roll pastry to a 13-inch (32 cm) circle; transfer to large baking sheet. Using a sharp knife, trim pastry edge to form an even circle.

3. Filling: Starting 2 inches (5 cm) from edge, overlap apple slices in a circle; arrange another overlapping circle of apples in center. In a bowl combine sugar, pecans and cinnamon; sprinkle over apples. Fold pastry rim over apples to form a 2-inch (5 cm) edge.

4. Bake for 35 to 40 minutes or until pastry is golden and apples are tender. Place on rack; let cool. With a spatula, carefully slide pie onto serving platter.

FROM
Fast & Easy Cooking
by Johanna Burkhard

Individual Apple Strudel

Serves 6

Phyllo dough works so well for strudel, you'd swear the stuff was invented for it. I've enriched this basic recipe with pecans, which lend a sun-belt warmth that is particularly welcome when this dessert is served in winter.

Leftovers can be kept covered and unrefrigerated. Warm slightly before serving.

Use any variety of apples. To avoid browning, add the apple slices to the orange-lemon juice immediately after peeling and slicing.

FROM
The New Vegetarian Gourmet
by Byron Ayonoglu

PREHEAT OVEN TO 350° F (180° C)
BAKING SHEET, LIGHTLY GREASED WITH BUTTER

1/4 cup	orange juice	50 mL
1 tbsp	lemon juice	15 mL
1 lb	apples, peeled, cored and cut into thin slices	500 g
2 tbsp	cornstarch	25 mL
1 cup	toasted pecans	250 mL
1/3 cup	raisins	75 mL
3 tbsp	brown sugar	45 mL
1 tsp	ground cinnamon	5 mL
1/2 tsp	ground nutmeg	2 mL
1/2 tsp	ground clove	2 mL
12	sheets phyllo dough	12
1/2 cup	melted unsalted butter	125 mL

1. In a bowl mix together orange and lemon juices. Add apple slices, stirring to coat with juice. Sprinkle apples with cornstarch; mix well. Add pecans, raisins, sugar, cinnamon, nutmeg, and clove; mix gently but thoroughly.

2. On a dry surface lay out a sheet of phyllo; brush with melted butter. Cover with a second sheet of phyllo; brush with butter. Transfer one-sixth apple mixture (about 3/4 cup [175 mL]) to upper center of buttered phyllo sheet. Fold top flap over filling; fold both vertical sides to inside, as if shaping an envelope. Roll stuffed end down to create a plump rectangular pie, measuring about 4 by 2 inches (10 by 5 cm). Transfer pie to baking sheet; repeat filling procedure for 5 remaining pies. Brush remaining melted butter on tops and sides of pies.

3. Bake in preheated oven for 15 to 20 minutes or until phyllo is golden brown and crisp. Remove from oven; let cool at least 10 minutes before serving.

Peanutty Cereal Snacking Bars

Makes 24 bars

Peanut butter fans will love these no-bake bars. They're a breeze to make and taste so much better than those expensive packaged snack bars. Also, they make a nice change from that other popular snack for kids — Rice Krispie squares.

TIP

Wrap bars individually in plastic wrap and then freeze.When making school lunches, just pop a pre-wrapped bar into each lunch bag.

FROM
The Comfort Food Cookbook
by Johanna Burkhard

13- BY 9-INCH (3.5 L) BAKING PAN, GREASED

1 cup	smooth or chunky peanut butter (regular or light)	250 mL
2/3 cup	honey *or* golden corn syrup	150 mL
4 cups	toasted rice cereal	1 L
2 cups	muesli-type cereal with fruit and nuts	500 mL

1. In a large saucepan combine peanut butter and honey; cook over medium heat, stirring constantly, until smooth. (Or place in large glass bowl and microwave, stirring once, at High for 2 minutes or until smooth.)

2. Fold in cereal until evenly coated. Press firmly into prepared baking pan. Let cool; cut into 3- by 1 1/2-inch (8 by 4 cm) bars.

Makes about 18 pancakes

Buttermilk Flapjacks

Cowboys in the Old West couldn't count on having maple syrup on the table for their morning pancakes. Many just slopped on some "Charlie Taylor" — a sweet mixture of bacon grease and molasses that took the place of syrup.

5 cups	all-purpose flour	1.25 L
3 tbsp	granulated sugar	45 mL
2 tsp	baking soda	10 mL
1 tsp	baking powder	5 mL
3 cups	buttermilk	750 mL
2 cups	half-and-half (10%) cream	500 mL
5	eggs, beaten	5
1/4 cup	melted butter	50 mL
1 tsp	vanilla	5 mL

1. In a large bowl, stir together flour, sugar, baking soda and baking powder.

2. In another bowl, whisk together buttermilk, half-and-half cream, eggs, butter and vanilla. Add to flour mixture, stirring until smooth.

3. Spoon batter onto a hot greased griddle or seasoned cast iron pan; cook until bubbles form on one side. Flip pancakes; brown the second side. Serve immediately.

FROM
The Wild West Cookbook
by Cinda Chavich

Dark Chocolate Layer Cake with Rich Chocolate Frosting

You'll be amazed to discover that this fabulous chocolate cake is as easy to bake as a store-bought mix. It makes a very special birthday treat for friends and family.

TIP

To melt chocolate, place in a metal bowl; set over a saucepan of simmering water until melted. Or, place in a glass bowl; microwave at Medium for 2 1/2 to 3 1/2 minutes. Let cool slightly.

For easy clean-up, place strips of waxed paper around bottom cake layer prior to frosting. When cake is frosted, pull strips away.

FROM
The Comfort Food
Cookbook
by Johanna Burkhard

PREHEAT OVEN TO 350° F (180° C)
TWO 9-INCH (2.5 L) ROUND CAKE PANS, GREASED AND FLOURED, BOTTOMS LINED WITH PARCHMENT OR WAXED PAPER

Cake

2 cups	all-purpose flour	500 mL
1 1/2 tsp	baking soda	7 mL
1/2 tsp	baking powder	2 mL
1/2 tsp	salt	2 mL
1/2 cup	butter, at room temperature	125 mL
1 1/2 cups	granulated sugar	375 mL
4 oz	unsweetened chocolate, melted	125 g
2	large eggs	2
1 1/2 cups	buttermilk	375 mL
2 tsp	vanilla	10 mL

Rich Chocolate Frosting

1/3 cup	butter, softened	75 mL
3 oz	unsweetened chocolate, melted and cooled	90 g
3 cups	icing sugar	750 mL
1 tsp	vanilla	5 mL
1/3 cup	milk (approximate)	75 mL

1. In a bowl stir together flour, soda, baking powder and salt.

2. In another bowl using an electric mixer, cream butter and sugar until fluffy. Add melted chocolate, eggs, buttermilk and vanilla; beat until smooth. Add flour mixture; beat until smooth.

3. Spread batter evenly in prepared pans. Bake in preheated oven for 35 minutes or until cake tester inserted in center comes out clean. Cool on wire rack for 5 minutes. Run knife around edge; turn out onto wire racks. Cool completely.

Frosted cake can
be frozen.

4. In a bowl using an electric mixer, beat together butter and melted chocolate until smooth. Add icing sugar, vanilla and enough milk to make a smooth spreadable frosting; beat until smooth.

5. Place 1 cake layer onto serving plate. Spread with frosting. Top with second layer; spread frosting over top and sides of cake.

Makes about 4 dozen cookies

No-Fail Shortbread

The secret to this tender shortbread is not to overwork the dough, especially when kneading. For light cookies, sift the flour, then spoon into a metal measuring cup; level top using a knife.

PREHEAT OVEN TO 300° F (150° C)

1 cup	unsalted butter, softened	250 mL
1/2 cup	superfine sugar (fruit sugar)	125 mL
1 tsp	vanilla	5 mL
2 cups	sifted all-purpose flour	500 mL
1/4 tsp	salt	1 mL

1. In a bowl beat butter with a wooden spoon until fluffy; beat in sugar a little at a time until well blended. Beat in vanilla. Stir in flour and salt; shape dough into a ball. On a lightly floured board, gently knead 5 times or until smooth.

2. Divide dough into 4 pieces. On a lightly floured surface, roll each piece to 1/3-inch (8 mm) thickness; cut out shapes using cookie cutters. Place on ungreased baking sheets. Bake, one sheet at a time, in middle of preheated oven for 25 to 30 minutes or until edges are light golden.

FROM
Johanna Burkhard

a b c d e f g h

Makes 24 bars

Lunch-Box Oatmeal Raisin Bars

Ideal for school lunches, these chewy bars travel well. I like to package bars individually in plastic wrap, place in a covered container and freeze. It's so easy to pop a bar from the freezer into lunchbags or take them along for snacks.

TIP

Lining the baking pan with foil makes it a breeze to remove bars and ensures a fast clean-up.

PREHEAT OVEN TO 350° F (180° C)
13- BY 9-INCH (3.5 L) BAKING PAN, LINED WITH GREASED FOIL

2/3 cup	packed brown sugar	150 mL
1/3 cup	butter *or* margarine	75 mL
1/3 cup	golden corn syrup	75 mL
2 1/2 cups	rolled oats	625 mL
1/4 cup	all-purpose flour	50 mL
1/2 cup	raisins or chopped dried apricots	125 mL
1	large egg	1
1 tsp	vanilla	5 mL

1. In a glass bowl combine brown sugar, butter and corn syrup. Microwave at High for 2 minutes; stir until smooth. Microwave 1 minute or until sugar dissolves and mixture comes to a full boil.

2. Stir in rolled oats, flour and raisins. In a bowl beat egg and vanilla. Stir into rolled-oats mixture.

3. Spread evenly in prepared pan. Bake for 20 to 25 minutes or until golden around edges. Let cool 10 minutes in pan. Lift out foil; cut into 3- by 1 1/2-inch (8 by 4 cm) bars. Transfer to a rack; cool completely.

FROM
Fast & Easy Cooking
by Johanna Burkhard

Index

More of your favorite recipes

Robert Rose's Favorite
MEALS IN MINUTES

RECIPES SELECTED FROM BYRON AYANOGLU • JOHANNA BURKHARD • ANDREW CHASE
CINDA CHAVICH • BILL JONES • ROSE REISMAN • KATHLEEN SLOAN • STEPHEN WONG

ISBN 0-7788-0008-3

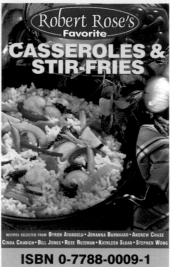

Robert Rose's Favorite
CASSEROLES & STIR-FRIES

RECIPES SELECTED FROM BYRON AYANOGLU • JOHANNA BURKHARD • ANDREW CHASE
CINDA CHAVICH • BILL JONES • ROSE REISMAN • KATHLEEN SLOAN • STEPHEN WONG

ISBN 0-7788-0009-1

Robert Rose's Favorite
LIGHT COOKING

RECIPES SELECTED FROM BYRON AYANOGLU • JOHANNA BURKHARD • PAT CROCKER
ROSE MURRAY • ROSE REISMAN • KATHLEEN SLOAN

ISBN 0-7788-0016-4

Robert Rose's Favorite
PASTA

RECIPES SELECTED FROM BYRON AYANOGLU • JOHANNA BURKHARD
ANDREW CHASE • BILL JONES • ROSE REISMAN • STEPHEN WONG

ISBN 1-896503-74-8

Robert Rose's Favorite
LIGHT DESSERTS

ISBN 1-896503-72-1

Robert Rose's Favorite
COOKIES CAKES & PIES

RECIPES SELECTED FROM BYRON AYANOGLU • JOHANNA BURKHARD
ANDREW CHASE • BILL JONES • ROSE REISMAN • STEPHEN WONG

ISBN 1-896503-71-3

Robert Rose's Favorite
SNACKS • SALADS & APPETIZERS

RECIPES SELECTED FROM BYRON AYANOGLU • JOHANNA BURKHARD
ANDREW CHASE • BILL JONES • ROSE REISMAN • STEPHEN WONG

ISBN 1-896503-51-9

Robert Rose's Favorite
SOUPS & STEWS

RECIPES SELECTED FROM BYRON AYANOGLU • JOHANNA BURKHARD
ANDREW CHASE • BILL JONES • ROSE REISMAN • STEPHEN WONG

ISBN 1-896503-69-1

Robert Rose's Favorite
CHICKEN

RECIPES SELECTED FROM BYRON AYANOGLU • JOHANNA BURKHARD
ANDREW CHASE • BILL JONES • ROSE REISMAN • STEPHEN WONG

ISBN 1-896503-53-5